Mr Takahashi
and other falling secrets

Sandra Thibodeaux

jute

Corrugated
IRON

Currency Press,
Sydney

CURRENCY PLAYS

First published in 2017
by Currency Press Pty Ltd,
PO Box 2287, Strawberry Hills, NSW, 2012, Australia
enquiries@currency.com.au
www.currency.com.au
in association with Corrugated Iron Youth Arts, Darwin

Copyright: *Mr Takahashi and Other Falling Secrets* © Sandra Thibodeaux, 2005, 2017.

Cataloguing-in-publication data for this title is available from the National Library of Australia website: www.nla.gov.au

Typeset by Dean Nottle for Currency Press.
Cover shows Haylee Wright.
Image by Jett Street. Cover treatment by Tim Cooke.

Currency Press acknowledges the Traditional Owners of the Country on which we live and work. We pay our respects to all Aboriginal and Torres Strait Islander Elders, past and present.

Contents

WARNING: Aboriginal and Torres Strait Islander readers are warned that this publication contains images of deceased persons.

Above: Darwin from the air (Government House and the Esplanade). NTAS, C Wilson, NTRS 3335, Item 285.

Below: Star Pictures. NTAS, C Wilson, NTRS 3335, Item 386.

Right: Chinatown, Cavenagh St, Darwin. NTAS, C Wilson, NTRS 3335, Item 10.

Foreword
Katrina Fong Lim

When Dr Sandra Thibodeaux presented me with her play, *Mr Takahashi*, she did not warn me that it would be quite so confronting. She presents intertwined stories, evoking a torrid era of wartime woes and race relations, in her own exceptional style. Her ability to tell the tale of what it was like to be 'Darwinese', to grow up in this unique multicultural community, is what is so confronting. It brings back memories of a Darwin past, of family stories of setting up business outside the Chinatown area, of iced lemon squash and sewing for soldiers. It provides the faint echoes of a community where the picture theatre was the social hub, providing a welcome break to the mundane living in a remote tropical outpost.

In this, the 75th year since the Bombing of Darwin, it is fitting that the play is part of the commemorations. Thank you Sandra, for lending your considerable talents to this story from a true Darwinese.

Katrina Fong Lim
Lord Mayor of Darwin

CAVENAGH ST. DARWIN.

Mr Takahashi and Other Falling Secrets was first produced by Corrugated Iron Youth Arts and JUTE Theatre Company at Brown's Mart Theatre, Darwin, on 15 February 2017, with the following cast:

RUBY	Chenoa Deemal
MRS AGNES LAMB / JOAN	Merrilee Mills
SISTER CONCEPTUA	Natalie Taylor
GRACE	Haylee Wright
MOTHER DOLORES	Kate Wyvill

Director, Suellen Maunder
Set and Props Designer, Simone Tesorieri
Costume and Props Designer, Simona Cosentini
Composer and Musical Director, Netanela Mizrahi
Lighting Designer, Rebecca Adams
Production Manager, Angus Robson
Stage Manager, Andi Egan

Japanese bomber planes. NTAS, GA Hodgins, NTRS 1361, Item 9.

CHARACTERS

MAGGIE TAKAHASHI, 13, Australian-born daughter of Mr Takahashi, the town's photographer, intelligent, mates with Kristina.

KRISTINA KOLCHAK, 13, ebullient but insecure, mates with Maggie.

DOLORES, a Catholic nun ('Mother'), older, reflective, haunted by her past.

CONCEPTUA, a Catholic nun ('Sister'), younger, the popular 'Sister Janet Mead' of the convent.

GIRLS, representative of the Stolen Generations. These girls are played by the ensemble (minus the nuns) as a chorus. Occasionally, an individual girl talks—this can be any of the actors taking turns to voice an individual opinion.

GRACE, young (perhaps 15), Indigenous maid at Government House, musical, painfully shy.

RUBY, older (perhaps 20), Indigenous maid at Government House, majestic, a rebel.

MRS AUSTIN LAMB (AGNES), Administrator's wife, bossy with grand ideas about herself but can be self-conscious, especially when dealing with Ruby. Her marriage is an empty shell.

JOAN CARROLL, postal worker and mother of Betty, attractive, fractured, heavy drinker, husband away at war.

BETTY CARROLL, postal worker, more practical than her mother and covers for her, misses her father.

ROSE CHIN, older sister, less attractive than Lily and resentful, has managed the family business since the death of their mother and is old before her time.

LILY CHIN, younger sister, gorgeous and dreamy.

Other roles are played by the chorus.

SETTING

Darwin between June 1941 and 19 February 1942. The play concludes with a scene set in May 1946.

The action takes place within family houses, workplaces and public areas. Space should be used fluidly and stylistically.

Garden Point is a Catholic mission on Melville Island, off the northern Australian coast. The nuns observe the lives of the Darwin characters in an omnipotent fashion.

Oil tanks burning. NTAS, R Urquhart, NTRS 258, Item 46.

The characters and events in this play are fictitious, and any resemblance to real persons, living or dead, is purely coincidental.

This play went to press before the end of rehearsals and may differ from the play as performed.

ACT ONE

Darwin, July 1941.

GIRLS: [*singing/chanting*] Over the garden wall,
    I let the baby fall.
    Then mother came out and gave me a clout,
    And sent me over the wall, the wall, the wall, the wall …

The GIRLS *continue to chant softly as a wind howls up from the south. It sounds like a baby wailing.*

Lights build on DOLORES, *who's on the verandah of the convent at Garden Point, investigating the day.* CONCEPTUA *comes out.*

CONCEPTUA: That's a Dry Season hymn …

DOLORES: Bold as brass, that wind. [*To the wind*] Bringing up the desert again?

CONCEPTUA: You should go inside, Mother.

DOLORES: The leaves are stripped …

CONCEPTUA: Shut the louvres.

DOLORES: It sneaks through the cracks.

CONCEPTUA: Close the curtains.

DOLORES: The curtains rip. The cradles—

CONCEPTUA: Rock, Mother. They rock.

Lights find MAGGIE *and* KRISTINA, *skipping.*

GIRLS: January, February, March, April, May, June …

MAGGIE *skips in double time.*

CONCEPTUA: There's Maggie Takahashi …

DOLORES: And her bosom friend, Kristina.

CONCEPTUA: Maggie's leaving Darwin. Take a photo, Mr Takahashi!

A light flashes.

GIRL: That camera gonna take her spirit, Sister. That camera gonna take her away!

GIRLS: No, it won't!

GIRL: Cover your face, sis!

The camera flashes.

CONCEPTUA: Your spirit, Maggie Takahashi, is in the hands of our Lord. A fine Catholic school it is …

KRISTINA: Why can't you go to a public school?

MAGGIE: Mum won't let me. You know what she'll say …

GIRLS: 'Public dogs sitting on logs, eating maggots out of frogs.'

DOLORES *clips the ear of the nearest* GIRL.

KRISTINA: Let's run up Chinatown, Maggie.

MAGGIE: I have to pack!

KRISTINA: I'll buy you some salty plums. Won't have *them* at your dried-up nunnery!

Arm-in-arm, they skip down Cavenagh Street, sweeping up treats from shops.

GIRLS: Wing Cheong Sing.
Wing Wah Loong.
Wing Sang Toy.
Fang Chong Loong.

KRISTINA: And the Chung King Café.

GIRLS: G.P. Wong.
C.P. Cheong.
Sun Hing Kee.
Yean Ying Bakery.

MAGGIE: [*awestruck*] And the Man Fong Lau. It's a bonza place. Like you see in the pictures!

KRISTINA: Mum says it's full of communists.

MAGGIE: Nah—KMT, Dad reckons.

KRISTINA: What's that?

MAGGIE: [*shrugging*] Something political …

KRISTINA: Must be communists. Chinamen are communists, eh?

MAGGIE: Nah, they're Confucius.

GIRLS: Restaurants:
Tung Fong.
Yuen Tung.
Nam King … and 'Tropical Views'.

The camera flashes.

KRISTINA: Not a great view for One-Eyed Kin, the owner!

MAGGIE: Nah …

KRISTINA: He's Japanese, eh?

MAGGIE: S'pose so …

    KRISTINA *glances at* MAGGIE.

KRISTINA: You're not but, are ya?

MAGGIE: I'm Australian.

KRISTINA: Yeah, like me.

MAGGIE: Yeah.

KRISTINA: And your mum's not a Jap?

MAGGIE: She's Catholic!

KRISTINA: Yeah, she's Catholic!

    Beat.

You don't look Japanese … really.

GIRLS: Kristina!

CONCEPTUA: Your mother's calling.

GIRL: She's a cheeky one, Sister—always whingein' 'bout Japanese.

GIRLS: Where Japanese?

DOLORES: In Japan, of course.

GIRL: Except for the Takahashis.

GIRLS: They're not Japanese!

GIRL: Yes, they are!

GIRLS: No, they're not!

GIRL: What are they, then?

    Pause.

CONCEPTUA: They're Darwinese!

GIRLS: Chinese, Japanese, what are these, they're Darwinese!

    Lights up on the Chins' shop.

    ROSE CHIN *draws the bolt on the door.* LILY *brings in a block of ice and starts chopping it.* ROSE *folds soldiers' uniforms.*

CONCEPTUA: The Chins are opening shop—

DOLORES: Fresh fruit and vegies—

CONCEPTUA: Hems and buttons and starch—

DOLORES: And their famous lemon squash.

CONCEPTUA: When they first set up in Smith Street, everyone told them:

ROSE: 'The Whites won't trade with you in Smith Street! You'll have to go to Chinatown!'

CHORUS: Ching Chong Chinaman velly velly sad, much aflaid, alla tlade, velly velly bad. 'Long cummy Whitey man makey shutty shop. Ching Chong Chinaman chop, chop—'

DOLORES: *But* they were wrong.

CONCEPTUA: The shop's a roaring success.

DOLORES: 'Go to Chinatown,' they said.

ROSE: Only to buy my duck!

> *The* CHORUS, *as soldiers, tramp down the street.*

> LILY *watches from the window.*

DOLORES: Here they come, the soldiers.

CONCEPTUA: Tramping down Smith Street like lords of the world.

> *A dog howls.*

CHORUS: [*roughly*] Come out, Lily Chin! I'll float your boat to China!

ROSE: Why don't you float back where you come from? [*Muttering*] Bloody Southerners … Lily—the lemons. Come on!

> LILY *returns to squeezing lemons. The dog howls.*

LILY: Lots of soldiers in town.

ROSE: Pictures.

LILY: Oh … You gonna sell things?

ROSE: Maybe peanuts.

LILY: Can I come?

ROSE: Too many fellas.

> *The dog howls.*

There's Charles from Yam Yan's. Gosh, he's tall … [*Calling out the door*] You coming in?

> *Her face falls.*

She's busy.

> ROSE *turns away from the door.*

LILY: What's on?

ROSE: *Hound of the Baskervilles.* This rich man ruins a pretty girl who runs away. So he sets the hounds after her. She ends up all bloody and rotten with maggots.

LILY: Horror?

ROSE: Comedy.

Lights crossfade to Government House.

GRACE is shelving the china, delicately. She holds a rose-painted teapot.

CONCEPTUA: Over at Government House, Grace is taking care with the china.

DOLORES: She's never broken one piece.

CONCEPTUA: Good morning, Grace!

GRACE: Good morning, Sister.

CONCEPTUA: She's such a—

AGNES: [*offstage*] Good Girl ...?

GRACE drops the pot in surprise. She pushes the pieces under a chair.

CONCEPTUA: Mrs Agnes Lamb—

DOLORES: The Administrator's wife.

CONCEPTUA: Even at this hour, she's dressed to the nines.

DOLORES: Stockings at all times—

CONCEPTUA: Hat and gloves for out-of-doors.

DOLORES: How she must burn!

AGNES swishes in, carrying a bright yellow frock.

AGNES: We're having our portraits taken today. Mr Takahashi.

A camera flashes.

Can you press this, please?

GRACE: The yellow one?

Beat.

AGNES: I'm holding *only* one frock, girl. It's ... cheery.

GRACE: Yes, missus—cheery.

AGNES: Too ... cheery?

Beat.

GRACE: Oh, no, no, no, madame—you look pretty in that one. Young.

AGNES *considers and puts the frock down.*

AGNES: I'll wear the brown one.

GRACE: It was too tight?

AGNES: [*sharply*] I thought you fixed it?

GRACE *looks away.*

[*Softening*] Do a good job, and I'll find you a surprise.

GRACE: Thank you, missus.

AGNES *goes into the dressing-room (offstage).*

AGNES: [*offstage*] That new girl is due today. Can you see that she's settled?

GRACE: Yes, madame.

AGNES: [*offstage*] And I'd like a cup of tea before I go. In that rose pot, thank you.

GRACE*'s face falls.*

[*Offstage*] Did you hear me, Good Girl?

GRACE: Yes, madame.

GRACE *grimaces, scoops up the china.*

CHORUS: [*singing/chanting*] Over the garden wall,
        I let the baby fall.
        Then mother came out and gave me a clout,
        And sent me over the wall, the wall, the wall, the wall …

Lights crossfade to a street where JOAN *wheels a pram out.*

She stops beside a gallon drum bin and drops a bottle in. Then she drops another and another …

DOLORES: Mrs Carroll!

A hungover JOAN *looks up, waves and smiles grimly.* BETTY *enters, smartly dressed.*

CONCEPTUA: Off to work, Betty?

BETTY: I got a promotion. Can't say but—

JOAN: War Office—all hush-hush.

BETTY: Mum …

JOAN: These young girls, you know? They run rings around us.

JOAN *suddenly plonks down, to* BETTY*'s surprise.*

DOLORES: Well, your father will be pleased …

BETTY *looks confused.*

CONCEPTUA: The promotion?

BETTY: Yeah, I hope so … [*To* JOAN] You right?

She hovers over her mother, a little impatiently.

CONCEPTUA: [*to* DOLORES] Poor girl. You know, he didn't come back for his leave.

DOLORES: I wouldn't leave Joan alone for long … that showgirl smile.

CONCEPTUA: She was an actress.

DOLORES: Much the same—lipstick and filth.

BETTY: Will I tell them you're sick?

JOAN: I'll be right in a minute.

BETTY: You look real crook.

JOAN: Well, pass me your compact.

BETTY: You're making me late!

She passes it reluctantly. JOAN *looks in the mirror.*

JOAN: My God. Who is this? And what did she do last night?

BETTY: It's the Witch of the West—and the same as *every* night.

JOAN *powders.*

JOAN: I'm sorry, lovey … I'll take you to the pictures later. Alright?

She holds the compact out. BETTY *grabs it, snaps it shut.*

BETTY: Let's just go.

Lights up on DOLORES, CONCEPTUA *and other relevant characters.*

DOLORES: All of the women are cutting.

CONCEPTUA: Our girls are snipping out paper angels.

DOLORES: Why do the angels fall?

A baby wails.

CONCEPTUA: Hush now, Mother.

The wailing fades.

DOLORES: Kristina hacks at the bougainvillea.

CONCEPTUA: Betty censors mail—

DOLORES: Butchering secrets—

CONCEPTUA: Wives to their husbands; soldiers to brothers; and Good-Girl Grace to her sweetheart, Francis, who sailed away on a Japanese pearler and was never heard of again.

DOLORES: And what does the censored version say?

BETTY: [*reading*] 'Dear Francis. I hope this finds you … Still here. I hear there are sharks? I'm at … Seems like a long time ago. The mission. The dark. You brought me plums. Said you were going off to find me some …'

GRACE: Have you found a new love?

DOLORES: Love is a jail; Grace is a prisoner.

CHORUS: [*singing*] I wrote a letter to my love and on the way I dropped it.

CONCEPTUA: Incoming, Betty … postmarked Hong Kong.

Like Chinese Whispers, the CHORUS *pass a letter to* BETTY, *who goes to open it.*

DOLORES: It's addressed to Mrs Carroll.

BETTY: But it must be from Dad …?!

CONCEPTUA: Never open people's letters.

DOLORES: We know you're not Catholic, but …

BETTY *is tempted by the letter, then drops it.*

CHORUS: [*singing*] Someone must have picked it up and put it in their pocket …

CONCEPTUA: Listen …

Pause.

Rose is at it: snip, snip, snip.

GIRLS: What's she making, Sister?

CONCEPTUA: A pretty pink dress for Good-Girl Grace.

DOLORES: A gift from Mrs Lamb.

GIRL: Is she gonna go to the pictures?

GIRLS: She's not allowed!

CONCEPTUA: She's got an exemption—

GIRL: For being a good girl!

Lights up on GRACE, *rushing to the servants' quarters with a jar of make-up in her hands. She stops at the door, opens and smells it. Then she notices* RUBY, *seated like a queen inside.*

RUBY: What's that you got?

GRACE *hesitates.*

GRACE: Are you the new girl?
RUBY: Yeah.
GRACE: I'm Grace … and … the missus asked me to show you things.
RUBY: Oh, yeah. Show me *that* thing, Grace.

GRACE *hands her the cream.*

Charmosan Hand Lotion … You get this from the missus?
GRACE: No, it's mine … I have to put it away.
RUBY: It's alright if I use it first?

RUBY *opens the jar and uses the cream while* GRACE *looks on anxiously.*

GRACE: It's expensive …
RUBY: I'll put it away.
GRACE: No!

RUBY *has already opened* GRACE*'s drawer.*

RUBY: Lord, what you got in here!

She pulls out and investigates various pots.

GRACE: My creams and things—don't!

AGNES *barges in with another jar. She's wearing a yellow hat.*

AGNES: I've found another one almost finished … [*Noticing* RUBY] Hello? You must be the new girl? I'm the Administrator's wife—Mrs Lamb.

RUBY *stands, towering over* AGNES.

RUBY: Madame …

RUBY *curtsies.*

AGNES: Did Grace … show you everything?
GRACE: I was gonna—
AGNES: *Going* to, Grace.
RUBY: I'll need a duty list, madame, and a schedule.
AGNES: Oh, yes …? Nice to see someone pronouncing it correctly—
RUBY: 'Schedule', Madame.
GRACE: 'Schedule'.

AGNES: [*condescendingly*] Thank you, Grace.

> *Beat.*

Anyway, mustn't chat. [*To* GRACE] Here's the make-up, Girl—milk tone.

> *She hands it to* GRACE.

GRACE: Thank you.

> AGNES *turns to leave.*

RUBY: Nice hat, madame.

AGNES: Thank you …

RUBY: Ruby.

AGNES: Thank you, Ruby.

> *She goes to walk out the door.*

RUBY: But that frock, madame.

AGNES: Yes …?

RUBY: You need … a yellow one … maybe with a square neckline.

> AGNES *looks in the mirror, doubtfully.*

AGNES: Grace said it was alright.

RUBY: She's just a blackfella.

AGNES: Well, I don't have time to change now. Ruby, come and see me after lunch. Maybe you can be my special adviser!

> *She leaves.*

> RUBY *plonks down in front of the mirror.*

RUBY: Sorry, Sis. Wanna wear some 'milk tone' …?

> *Lights up on* DOLORES, CONCEPTUA *and other relevant characters.*

DOLORES: All of the women are preening.

CONCEPTUA: Pretty Lily combs lemon juice through her hair.

DOLORES: Coconut oil for Ruby.

CONCEPTUA: A final glance in the mirror for Mrs Agnes Lamb.

DOLORES: A final chance to finish off head lice for Maggie.

CONCEPTUA: All clear, Kristina?

KRISTINA: All clear!

MAGGIE: Phew! I'd die if I took nits down there—those Brisbane kids would scream.

KRISTINA: Wish I was going to Brisbane.

MAGGIE: I wish you were, too.

KRISTINA: Who am I gonna play with?

MAGGIE: I'll be back in the holidays—alright? And I'll write to you—
long letters.

KRISTINA: You'll forget about me.

MAGGIE: No, I won't.

KRISTINA: Maggie, what if you change?

Beat.

You might go all 'lah-di-dah' at the nunnery.

MAGGIE: It's a *school*. And I won't. Promise.

KRISTINA: Hey, Mags … you wanna be blood sisters?

MAGGIE: [*uncertain*] Yeah …

KRISTINA: Prick your thumb. Here …

She grabs some bougainvillea, pricks MAGGIE*'s thumb with a
thorn.*

MAGGIE: Ouch!

KRISTINA: Now, I'll prick mine.

She pricks.

Then … we mix the blood.

MAGGIE: I'm Catholic!

KRISTINA: Yeah …? Catholics don't have germs! That's the communists.

She presses her thumb to MAGGIE*'s.*

MAGGIE: I'm a bit scared, Kristina …

KRISTINA: The nuns won't know!

DOLORES/CONCEPTUA: Oh, really?!

Beat.

MAGGIE: No … about … I have to get on the boat—by myself—and—

KRISTINA: Yeah, but you'll be alright now! You've got my blood.

MAGGIE: Yeah?

KRISTINA: We're part of each other now—sisters … best friends forever.

MAGGIE *smiles.*

MAGGIE: Amen.

Lights up on the post office where JOAN *sorts the mail into two piles—'Darwin' and 'Other'. With each 'Darwin', she takes a swig from a long-neck.*

JOAN: Darwin … other place … Darwin, other, other, everywhere else, the rest of the world … Darwin!

BETTY *enters with a pot of soup.*

BETTY: Are you okay …?

JOAN: Dandy. Darwin … [*pointing to the pile*] civilisation … [*pointing*] that's you—your pile for the knife.

She demonstrates a knife slitting a throat.

BETTY: We were going to see *The Hound* …?

JOAN: Right. Horror?

BETTY *sighs.*

I'm a bit tired, Betts. Darwin!

She swigs.

BETTY: Here's some soup.

She puts the food out.

Did you hear any news?

JOAN: News? Well … there are whispers about Takahashi.

She taps her nose, secretively.

BETTY: I mean about Dad.

JOAN *looks blank.*

I thought you got a letter today?

JOAN: No?

BETTY: From Hong Kong?

Beat.

JOAN: That's right! Well … it wasn't much—more of a note, really—to tell me he's, you know, still got a head! He said to give you a kiss.

BETTY: Yeah?

JOAN: He was very proud of your promotion.

BETTY: Oh, really? Can I read it?

JOAN: No! I mean … it's at home. I left it at lunch. Are you checking my mail?

BETTY: Sorry. Of course not. No! And I only check outbound, anyway.

> *Pause.*

It's just … I only got that scabby postcard.

JOAN: Oh, Betts … He's on a ship, baby?

BETTY: So?

JOAN: It's a long swim to the mailbox?

BETTY: Other dads send letters!

JOAN: Billy's not 'other dads'—he was never one for the 'chinwag'.

BETTY: *Chinwag?!* Doesn't he miss me?

JOAN: Of course!

> *Beat.*

He's just … not … literate!

BETTY: Mum!

JOAN: Shall we teach him how to write …?

> *She grabs a pen and paper.*

Dear Dad, *this* is a letter. And these are letters I'm writing on my letter … I hope that doesn't confuse you …?

> BETTY *smiles.*

Let's go to the pictures. You need some cheering up.

> *She swigs at her beer.*

Wear that rose frock of yours. It brings out your colour.

BETTY: You sure you're alright?

JOAN: Good as gold. Last sip. [*She slugs it back*] No more. I'll wait here while you go change.

> BETTY *leaves.*

> JOAN *carefully withdraws a letter from a hiding place. She opens it, takes a brief look. Then she pops it down her bra.*

CHORUS: Someone must have picked it up and put it in their pocket …

> *Lights up on the maids' bedroom at Government House.*

> GRACE *sits before the mirror. Her face is smeared with make-up, and she's not entirely happy with the effect. So she slaps on a bit more, and a bit more. Just as she's finishing,* RUBY *turns the door handle.* GRACE *hops into bed and pulls up the sheet.*

RUBY: Grace … You comin' to the pictures?

She shakes her gently.

You're not asleep, Girl! Come on.

She pulls on the tight sheet.

Come on, Gracey …

She yanks her out and laughs loudly.

Oh, dear Lord! You're as white as the missus' arse!

GRACE: Stop it!

GRACE flops back to bed.

RUBY: You look like you're dead! I'm gonna call you 'Ghost Girl' now … 'Ghostey'. Get up, Ghostey. Come on—time to go.

GRACE: I'm not comin'.

RUBY: Ghostey …

GRACE: Go away.

RUBY: Ah, come on, Grace. 'Course I'm gonna laugh—you look funny!

GRACE sits up.

GRACE: I look like Joan Crawford! What would you know? You're just a blackfella!

RUBY: Well, I know something … She's got you wrapped around her little finger—her and her used-up creams.

GRACE: No, she hasn't!

RUBY: I wouldn't take her scabby jars.

GRACE: They're nice! And they're my only things …

Beat.

RUBY: Come here, Gracey …

She starts cleaning GRACE's face.

You don't need her make-up. Look! You've got a beautiful face.

GRACE: No, I don't. My eye's wonky … I'm too dark.

RUBY: So's honey … You want them bees buzzing around? Come on. Picture's started.

Lights up on the Star Picture Theatre.

A camera flashes as LILY walks down the aisles, a tray of peanuts poised at her breasts. ROSE *is selling lollies. The newsreel begins, and the sisters hurry back to their seats.*

CHORUS: A people's war is being waged in China. Guerrillas in every village are working behind the lines to repel the Japanese. Using home-made grenades and Molotov cocktails …

ROSE: What did the soldiers want?

LILY: [*shrugging*] My name, how old I am …

ROSE: Too young!

CHORUS: Shhhh!

LILY: I sold lots of peanuts.

ROSE: I *knew* this would happen! We can't go anywhere without getting humbug. It's like you're the queen.

LILY: Princess.

ROSE: What?

LILY: They said I was a princess.

She beams innocently. ROSE *groans. Everyone turns around.*

CHORUS: Shhhh!

LILY: Charles is down there …

ROSE: I know. I saw him.

LILY: I thought you liked him?

ROSE: I did.

LILY: Maybe he likes you, too?

ROSE: He prefers *you.*

Beat.

I've been waiting ten years for you kids to get off my back.

LILY: I'm big now, Rosey—I'm right.

ROSE: You're still a child. And I'm becoming the Smith Street Spinster …

ROSE *shifts the tray of goodies and accidentally spills aniseed balls that clatter down the aisle.*

CHORUS: Oy!

The film slows and keeps clicking as it rotates. The lights die.

DOLORES: Something's wrong—the air is shifting.

CONCEPTUA: It's waiting …

DOLORES: Waiting for the tardy storms.

CONCEPTUA: You could cut the humidity—

DOLORES: With the sword of a samurai.
CONCEPTUA: Where *are* the Japanese?
CHORUS: Closer.
DOLORES: In June, they were in—
CHORUS: China.
DOLORES: In July, they swooped down over—
CHORUS: French Indochina.
CONCEPTUA: Now, Hong Kong's in their sights.
DOLORES: It's August and the land is waiting.

An air-raid siren sounds. The lights dim on Star Pictures.

RUBY: What?!
GRACE: It's that air-raid test.
RUBY: Bugger. How long's it for?
GRACE: [*shrugging*] An hour …
RUBY: Eh?! They already tested the siren.

> *Beat.*

You wanna smoke?
GRACE: We can't—no lights!

> RUBY *sighs.*

RUBY: I'm goin' outside.
GRACE: Stay here, Rube—I'm frightened.
RUBY: What for?
GRACE: It's dark and … quiet. What if they come?
RUBY: The Japs?! They're a long way away! You're myall*!

> *She goes to get up.*

GRACE: I'm not gettin' up in front of them white mob!
RUBY: *I* am. Gonna find me a big, strong soldier.

> RUBY *leaves.*

GRACE: Sis!

> *The air-raid siren sounds. Lights crossfade to* KRISTINA, *sitting on her bed. She lights a candle, and begins a letter. Music underscores her thoughts.*

---

* A derogatory term for someone from the bush who's not familiar with town ways.

KRISTINA: Dear Maggie, you should've been here! We had our first blackout tonight. It was eerie. The air-raid siren wailed like a wounded dingo. We had to turn out the lights, and pretend the Japanese were coming—not *you*; the real Japanese. It gave me the shivers.

Lights up on the post office where BETTY *censors the letter with scissors.*

BETTY: Dear Maggie, you should've been here! We had a black night. The air wailed like a wounded dingo.

CHORUS: [*singing*] Cut lights and the Japanese—
    You, Japanese.
    You gave me the shivers.

KRISTINA: How's school? Are the girls nice? I hope you're having a great time. You still coming back in December?

CHORUS: [*singing*] Nice girls and the Japanese—
    You, Japanese.
    You gave me the shivers.

KRISTINA: I went to your father's studio. It was Mum's idea—get a portrait done for my birthday. He's got a lot of mirrors, hey? It's to check your hair, they reckon.

BETTY: I checked on your father. It was Mum, full of ideas. A portrait, a lot of mirrors, smoke and mirrors and suspicious mail.

KRISTINA: You know, I have to ask you something … I mean, I don't think it's true or anything, but is your father a spy? The newspaper says that:

KRISTINA/BETTY: 'Traitors deserve death'!

KRISTINA: Maybe you should—

KRISTINA/BETTY: Stop being Japanese—

KRISTINA: So you don't get into trouble. Can't you—

KRISTINA/BETTY: Change your name—

KRISTINA: Or something? I remain your best friend—

KRISTINA/BETTY: Forever and ever—

KRISTINA: Blood sisters until the end.

The lights cut out. A window shatters, a dog makes a racket, the CHORUS *(as soldiers) stamp down the street.*

CONCEPTUA: *The Hound of the Baskervilles* has been released.

DOLORES: The hunt has just begun.

CONCEPTUA: They're boys ruining uniforms.

DOLORES: They're dogs on the run.

CHORUS: [*singing roughly*] Ten yellow bastards sitting on the wall …

> *Beneath the following dialogue, the* CHORUS *continues to sing.*
>
> *Dim light on Chins' shop where* ROSE *stands in the doorway. The dog is howling.*

ROSE: Lily?!

CHORUS: [*singing*] Lily, won't you blow, Lily, won't you blow …

> ROSE *shuts the door. A bottle smashes outside. The singing continues.*

DOLORES: Where's your sister, Rose …?

CONCEPTUA: Your mother is rolling in her grave!

ROSE: Still at the pictures.

CONCEPTUA: Lord have mercy!

ROSE: I got sick of it—it's like she's a film star!

DOLORES: And you *left* her there!

CHORUS: [*singing*] Someone's in the kitchen with Lily, someone's in the kitchen I know-o-o …

> ROSE *opens the door.*

ROSE: [*yelling*] Lily!

> *She closes the door again.*

Please—I didn't mean to …

CONCEPTUA: We'll offer up prayers.

DOLORES: Intercede.

CONCEPTUA/DOLORES: Hail Mary, full of grace, the Lord is with—

> LILY *bursts in the back door, all smiles.*

ROSE: Where have you been?

LILY: You should've seen—this beautiful, beautiful man with wild, green eyes …

> ROSE *slaps her roughly, a few times.*

CHORUS: [*chanting*] Long cummy whitey man,
　　　　Makey shutty shop.
　　　　Ching Chong Chinaman,
　　　　Chop, chop, chop.

A window breaks. The girls run behind the counter. There are smashing sounds, yells.

CONCEPTUA: Lily hides amongst the lemons.

DOLORES: Soldiers divide the spoils and spoil the stock.

CONCEPTUA: They finger, filch—

CONCEPTUA/DOLORES: Pinch, flog—

ROSE: Things that don't belong to them!

She stands up with a shotgun; loads and shoots.

Get out, you mongrels!

She shoots again.

CHORUS: Ow! You bloody chink!

ROSE: Next time I won't miss!

CHORUS: [*from a distance*] Slanty-eyed bitch! Why don't you go back where you come from?

ROSE: Why don't *you*?

She shoots again. The dog howls.

You tell 'em, Yellow Peril.

The noises fade. LILY *creeps out.*

ROSE: You alright?

LILY *nods.*

LILY: [*breaking*] I saw that beautiful man with the wild, green eyes.

Beat.

He called us Chinks!

ROSE: Don't worry about it, Lily. Charles was there, too!

LILY: Hey, Rose—they wrote something …

She walks over to the window.

'Come and get it'?

A bass line marches.

CONCEPTUA: Can you stand the attention
        Drawn to a damaged shop?

DOLORES: These soldiers claim affection,
        Then spoil your wares, chop, chop, chop.

CHORUS: [*singing/chanting*] The enemy comes to the Territory.
Enemies go with the territory.
Whose is the territory?
Where's the enemy?
We crossed the wire into enemy fire—
Chop, chop, chop.

Lights up on the post office.

BETTY *and* JOAN *are reading the newspaper.*

BETTY: The Labor Party said:
CHORUS: 'Dissatisfaction with conditions triggered the riot.'
JOAN: Oh, poor dears. Flat beer?
CHORUS: Incoming!

Like Chinese whispers, the CHORUS *pass mailbags to the post office.* BETTY *and* JOAN *simultaneously grab for the first one.*

JOAN: It's *my* job, Betty …?

BETTY *relinquishes and returns to the paper while* JOAN *sorts mail.*

BETTY: There's a story on the Japanese:
CHORUS: 'His skin is different, his brain is different, his soul is entirely different from the white man's.'
JOAN: What about Takahashi? His brain's alright.
BETTY: Maybe *too* right. People are suspicious.
JOAN: What people—Kristina's mum? She's a few cards short of a deck.
BETTY: She wanted to report him—said he's sending Morse code to the Japs.
JOAN: Dot dot splat—save our brains?
BETTY: Well, he *does* have that mirror …

A spotlight on KRISTINA.

KRISTINA: [*to* CONCEPTUA] Sister, are Japanese souls really different?
CONCEPTUA: Kristina! If you don't have anything nice to say …
KRISTINA: But are they?
DOLORES: Is Maggie's?
KRISTINA: She's Catholic.
DOLORES: Well, then …
KRISTINA: They just give me the creeps, you know?

DOLORES/CONCEPTUA: Kristina!

KRISTINA: Not the Takahashis—the *real* Japanese. What about China? I saw a photo of these people—women, too—and they had blindfolds on, and the Japs were pushing them down this hole …

DOLORES: Where did you see this?

Beat.

KRISTINA: Mr Takahashi's …

Lights up on MAGGIE *in her school bedroom*

MAGGIE: Dear Kristina, almost holidays! I can't wait to see you again! What's it like? Is it dreadfully hot? I've grown used to cooler weather down here. What are you doing for Christmas? Come to the beach. I hope it storms! Remember how we used to sit on the cliffs, and watch them roll in? We'd count the gaps between the lightning and thunder, remember? Then we'd scream and run when it got too close! Anyway … my ship gets in on the twentieth of December. How was Pearl Harbour, hey? I can't believe those Japanese! Will you meet me at the wharf?

The lights fade. Distant thunder

DOLORES: A praying mantis is clinging to the door.

CONCEPTUA: We'll have a storm by three.

DOLORES: Where are the girls?

CONCEPTUA: Down in the mangroves.

DOLORES: Call them in … That's the wind that comes before the storm.

Thunder rolls, lights fade.

A plane approaches as the CHORUS *skips, singing:*

CHORUS: [*singing/chanting*] June, July, August, September, October, November.

The thunderous plane suddenly cuts.

[*Newsreel-style*] Citizens of Darwin … The Federal War Cabinet has ruled women and children must be compulsorily—

DOLORES: Compulsorily?

CHORUS: —evacuated by ship as soon as possible except those in essential services.

BETTY: I'm essential!

CONCEPTUA: Betty's essential.

DOLORES: Her mother's 'licentious'.

JOAN: And *that's* damned 'libellous'.

> *Beat.*

I'm not leaving my baby here.

CONCEPTUA: Joan has 'war duties' now, Mother.

DOLORES: Hmph—entertaining soldiers?

CONCEPTUA: No—her showgirl days are over.

DOLORES: Along with her reputation.

ROSE: Hey, Canberra—evacuate *this*!

> *She makes a rude gesture with her rolled-up paper.*

CONCEPTUA: Now, Rose, if you can't say anything nice …

DOLORES: Besides, the shop is essential. She can stay and suffer with the rest.

CONCEPTUA: But, Mother—there's Lily to consider … It's hardly a place for young girls.

GRACE: Missus, I *wanna* go?!

AGNES: We're essential, girl.

GRACE: But the Japs are coming!

RUBY: Your fundraising dance—essential.

AGNES: Essential! The Red Cross need a new wireless.

GRACE: Everyone else is going!

AGNES: Well, the *captain* … goes down with the ship. We shall stay with our subjects and keep them / safe.

RUBY: Dancing.

> *They look at each other.*

CHORUS: Citizens greatly assist by cheerfully complying.

> *Lights up on the Chins' shop.* ROSE *and* LILY *are glumly considering options with a newspaper nearby.*

LILY: We've only just fixed up the shop …

ROSE: I'm not going anywhere.

LILY: Hey?

ROSE: You can go if you like. Go …

LILY *sighs.*

Mum worked her guts out all those years—the only Chinese in the street. No-one would buy from us! But she won that war. And no idiot soldier's gonna wreck this place again.

LILY: But you're not invincible.

ROSE: You go if you like. [*Softer*] Maybe you should go.

Pause.

I'm gonna start the trench …

She goes to the door.

LILY: Somebody nicked our shovel.

ROSE: Mongrels!

LILY: There's lots for sale but.

ROSE: Probably *ours*!

LILY *passes the newspaper to* ROSE *as we hear agitated music.*

[*Rhythmically*] 'For sale: double bedroom suite, dining table, ice chest, six good chairs and *three shovels.*'

LILY: Yes! 'Gramophone, fowl house, thirty-five young chickens, all good condition.'

ROSE: Chickens?!

A dog howls.

Perfect fertiliser.

ALL: [*singing/chanting*] 'Thirty-five young chickens, all good condition—'

GRACE: 'Pictures and a wireless!'

AGNES: Well spotted, Grace! We'll buy it, eh? 'Wireless, gents' lowboy—'

ALL: [*singing/chanting*] 'Thirty-five young chickens, all good condition—'

AGNES: 'Crockery, *piano*!'

GRACE: Piano!

Beat.

AGNES: If you're a good girl … I might go get it for you.

DOLORES: Half the town are selling up:

CONCEPTUA: 'A seagrass table, hall clock—'

ALL: [*singing/chanting*] 'Thirty-five young chickens, all good condition—'

DOLORES: 'A baby's bassinet—'

BETTY: And look, Mum: 'A Hawaiian steel guitar!' Dad would love it!

The music stops.

JOAN: Oh, dear … there's a Kodak Retina camera and enlarger for sale …

A ship's horn blows.

CHORUS: There will be hardship and sacrifice.

CONCEPTUA: Personal effects must not exceed thirty-five pounds.

DOLORES: Cheerfulness extra …

Lights up on KRISTINA, *who is packing and very upset.*

KRISTINA: I don't even know where we're going?! What should I pack?!

DOLORES: Thirty-five pounds.

CONCEPTUA: Only your precious things, dear … and a warm jumper.

KRISTINA: Where we going?

CONCEPTUA: Somewhere safe.

DOLORES: But probably cold.

KRISTINA: Are we gonna come back?

CONCEPTUA: Of course you'll come back.

KRISTINA: How long will it be?

DOLORES: Silence! You're dragging those heels …

CONCEPTUA: Put a smile on that lovely face.

DOLORES: You'll trip on that bottom lip!

KRISTINA: Stop being mean!

Beat.

Maggie's coming home today …?

DOLORES: Maggie?!

Pause.

CHORUS: Takahashi?!

Pause.

DOLORES: Your port, girl?

KRISTINA *opens her case.*

CONCEPTUA: They won't let you take all of that, dear.

CONCEPTUA *pulls out several things and then closes it firmly.*
KRISTINA *takes the port and leaves, bottom lip protesting.*

A ship's horn booms.

MAGGIE *enters, also holding a small case.*

CHORUS: Women and children, this way. Japanese down below. Japanese? Down below.
CONCEPTUA: She's just a girl.
DOLORES: Maggie Takahashi? Her name's on the list.
MAGGIE: Excuse me—I think there's been a mistake. I'm Australian.

Beat.

My mum's Catholic, you know. We've lived in Darwin for years! I go to St Maria Goretti in Brisbane. You ask the teachers—they'll tell you. I'm not Japanese!
CHORUS: [*slowly*] Chinese, Japanese, who are these—they're internees.

Pause.

Dirty internees.

The ship horn booms, fading into the distance. Lights crossfade to Government House.

AGNES *is dressed in a slip, examining her wardrobe.* RUBY *enters.*

AGNES: I think I'll wear the purple one.
RUBY: Purple?
AGNES: You don't think so?
RUBY: I don't know, madame … With your orange hair?
AGNES: Strawberry blonde!
RUBY: Sorry—strawberry.
AGNES: Blonde.

Beat.

Well, what do you suggest?

RUBY *selects a frock.*

RUBY: This black one.
AGNES: Do you think?

RUBY *pulls out the pieces as she speaks.*

RUBY: Jade necklace … green gloves and shoes.

AGNES: Oh.

RUBY: To calm down that orange strawberry.

AGNES *looks sharply at her, drops it.*

AGNES: It's a tad fancy for war time? .

RUBY: We need flash clothes to cheer us up! We need your *example*, madame.

AGNES: That's a point. We don't want people losing morale.

RUBY *starts dressing her.*

RUBY: I might … like to go to that dance one time.

AGNES: Oh, yes.

RUBY: Must be swish, eh? All them beautiful dresses.

AGNES: Well … they all *try*, you know—but no-one can match *your* style!

RUBY: Can't be, madame.

AGNES: As God is my witness!

Pause.

Any sign of Mr Lamb yet?

RUBY: Sorry—he said he'll meet you there.

AGNES: What?!

RUBY: He had a meeting—Air Raid Precautions?

AGNES: ARP? He *knew* it was my fundraiser?!

RUBY: [*shaking her head*] Men, hey … He should *move* that air raid.

AGNES: I've been planning this for months!

RUBY: Months, madame. I'll tell the driver to go and get him.

AGNES: Thank you, Ruby. At least, I can rely on *you* …

RUBY: You don't worry about a thing, madame. [*Shaking her head as she leaves*] ARP …

Planes murmur gently in the distance as lights crossfade to DOLORES *and* CONCEPTUA.

DOLORES: Fires will be started—

CONCEPTUA: And explosives set off around town.

CHORUS: [*newsreel-style*] During these tests, for your own protection, blackout and retire to your trenches.

CONCEPTUA: Rose has joined the ARP—

DOLORES: 'Asian Liaison'.

CONCEPTUA: She's inspecting all of the shops—

DOLORES: Starting with Yam Yan's.

The air-raid siren sounds. ROSE *barks instructions over the noise.*

ROSE: Where are your buckets, Charles? Two sand, two water; back door, front door. Move it, soldier.

The lights flicker, then go dim.

Call that a blackout, Charles? You'd be dead by now.

The lights flicker, go bright.

You've been randomly selected for an explosives test. We'll be dropping one on you tonight. *Do* make sure you're at home.

The siren winds down.

CONCEPTUA: She's taking it too far.

DOLORES: Put a uniform on someone … Here she goes with her 'grenades' …

LILY *and* ROSE *are practising with jam tins.*

ROSE: Lily, you're not playing cricket. Underarm, dingbat!

LILY: Like this?

ROSE: Yeah. Go for Charles's arse.

She lobs it.

CHORUS: Ow!

ROSE: [*calling out*] ARP test. As you were, soldier … [*To* LILY] Easy mistake—hard to tell his face from his arse, eh?! Come on—let's make some more.

They start to exit. A plane is heard swooping down. The GIRLS *stop still and watch it, squinting.*

Elsewhere, RUBY *also stops. Watches, squinting.*

The plane passes. They all retreat indoors.

RUBY *enters the maids' quarters, excitedly. She closes the door firmly behind her.*

RUBY: Alright, Grace—she's gone.

She strips to her underwear, dons a gorgeous red frock.

GRACE: They're not gonna let you in, you know?

RUBY: I've got my exemption … *and* a soldier. You should see him, Grace. Lovely!

GRACE: What if they ask you to leave?

RUBY: They won't.

GRACE: But it's Mrs Lamb's fundraiser. She'll get wild!

RUBY: She says I've got style. She reckoned I'm better than *all* that mob. How do I look?

GRACE: You look flash, but, Rube—

RUBY: Uh!

She sashays through the room like a model.

I've got my Wizard of Oz shoes!

GRACE: Shiny ones, sis.

RUBY: Who do I look like?

She adopts a dramatic pose.

GRACE: Judy Garland?

RUBY: She's just a kid! Scar-scar-scar—

GRACE: Scarecrow?

RUBY *glares.*

Scarlett O'Hara!

RUBY *blows a kiss.*

RUBY: [*in Scarlett accent*] I'll be back at dawn, most prob'ly …

RUBY *turns to go.*

GRACE: Ruby, have you gone silly? You'll get into trouble!

RUBY *halts at the doorway.*

RUBY: [*as Rhett*] Frankly, my dear, I don't give a damn …

She sweeps out, leaving GRACE *giddy at the whole idea. Lights flicker and waver, then crossfade to* DOLORES *and* CONCEPTUA.

DOLORES: The horizon isn't constant, you know. If you look very closely, there's always a wave.

CONCEPTUA: Mother?

DOLORES: There.

CONCEPTUA: That's not a wave—it's a ship.

DOLORES: It's a wave not returned.

CONCEPTUA: It's bearing the women to safety.

DOLORES: Spewing them to the end.

> *During the following, the* GIRLS *vomit intermittently.*

GIRLS: Bully beef, dog biscuits, brackish water, churning seas.

GIRL: Where all the kids going, Sister?

CONCEPTUA: Brisbane.

GIRLS: How come *we* never go on that ship?

CONCEPTUA: It's not your turn yet.

GIRL: When's *our* turn?

CONCEPTUA: Soon as they're ready.

DOLORES: Soon as the birds fall from the sky.

GIRL: They've got good swings in Brisbane!

DOLORES: [*drily*] Yes—they're making a slippery dip for you.

GIRL: Goody!

DOLORES: And putting in a pool.

CONCEPTUA: Stop it, Mother.

DOLORES: If we fell off the face of the earth, I doubt they'd even notice …

> *A baby wails. Lights up on* KRISTINA.

CONCEPTUA: Look, there's Kristina. That ship hasn't seen a mop and a broom in years!

DOLORES: It's overcrowded …

KRISTINA: Must be a thousand people!

CONCEPTUA: [*to* DOLORES] Too many. Do they have enough lifeboats? They look like chickens in a coop!

DOLORES: They look like bait.

> *Beat.*

KRISTINA: The cabins are stuffy. And you're not allowed to turn on the light!

CONCEPTUA: [*to* DOLORES] It's as dark as Davey Jones's locker.

DOLORES: Not quite—Mr Jones will be found down below with the internees.

> *Light on* MAGGIE.

See? There's Maggie. Locked in the hold …

CONCEPTUA: Someone should get her out! She's not Japanese!

GIRLS: [*slowly*] Chinese, Japanese, who are these? Japanese? Internees.

Pause.

Poor internees.

DOLORES: Birds are not nice. I watched two birds abandon a third. She was clearly struggling against the storm. What if she fell?

CONCEPTUA: Birds don't fall, Mother.

DOLORES considers.

DOLORES: I think it depends on the storm.

Lights brighten to reveal the deck.

CONCEPTUA: Once a day, they're released.

GIRLS: Exercise. One, two, one, two.

CONCEPTUA: In the blinding sun and the heat—

DOLORES: The hostility …

The CHORUS call 'Nip, Nip, Nip, Nip …' and random taunts such as 'Slanty eyes', 'Dirty Jap', etc. as MAGGIE walks past, trying to ignore them.

KRISTINA watches from a distance. MAGGIE spots her and dashes over.

MAGGIE: Kristina!

KRISTINA turns away.

KRISTINA: I can't talk.

MAGGIE: How come?

KRISTINA: You're an internee.

MAGGIE: But you know I'm not Japanese?!

KRISTINA: [*shrugging*] I don't know. Go away.

MAGGIE: Tina!

KRISTINA: Your name's Japanese … And you look Japanese, really.

MAGGIE: But I thought we were sisters—blood sisters!

KRISTINA: I didn't know you were Japanese back then.

MAGGIE: 'Cause I wasn't!

KRISTINA: What *were* you then?

MAGGIE: Australian!

KRISTINA: That's what you *told* me! But you keep on changing sides!

> *Beat.*

I know about your father.

MAGGIE: What?

KRISTINA: He's a spy.

MAGGIE: No, he's not!

KRISTINA: He's got that picture?

MAGGIE: What picture?

KRISTINA: Those Japs burying people alive. I saw it.

MAGGIE: [*unsure*] Maybe he wanted to keep it for … history or something.

KRISTINA: [*growing surer*] He was signalling with those mirrors.

MAGGIE: The *reflectors*?! They light the photographs—*your* photograph, remember?

> *Pause.*

KRISTINA: [*ashamed*] My mum sent me there …

MAGGIE: To stickybeak? My best friend!

KRISTINA: He was putting us in danger!

MAGGIE: He's not a spy—*you're* the dirty spy!

KRISTINA: You never saw him! You ran off to Brisbane. And look at you, Maggie—you've changed!

> KRISTINA *runs away.*

> *A distant air-raid siren. Dim lights on Government House.* RUBY *wanders into the girls' room, her red dress looking rumpled. She drops her shoes on the floor.*

GRACE: Ruby …?

> RUBY *doesn't talk, just sits and stares.*

How was … the dance?

> RUBY *nods for a while, then shrugs.*

RUBY: Alright.

> *Beat.*

Can you go?

> GRACE *leaves, fearfully. Then* RUBY *starts to groan. The groan gets louder as she throws her shoes across the room. She picks up*

one thing and another—throwing, tearing, smashing, and so on. She overturns chairs, rips the drawer out of the dressing table and hurls the make-up jars against the wall. After everything is ruined, she stands there, heaving. GRACE *creeps back in and watches.*

GRACE: What happened, sis'?

RUBY comes to. She packs a few things into a case.

Where you goin'?

RUBY doesn't answer, goes to the door.

Don't leave! Don't worry about her, Rube. She probably don't mean it!

RUBY: In front of everybody, Grace—all them high nobs! Didn't have the guts to do it herself! She told the sergeant. He took me out. I wished I could die!

GRACE: Please don't go—we'll fix it up tomorrow.

RUBY: I don't need to fix it! They can all go to hell! They want us to clean their mess and wash their stinking clothes but they don't want *us*! They wish we'd all disappear …

She walks into the darkness.

END OF ACT ONE

ACT TWO

SCENE ONE

Darwin, December 25, 1941.

The GIRLS *sing a delicate rendition of 'Away in a Manger'. (The children take breaths randomly as marked by the dashes.)*

GIRLS: [*singing*] Away in–a manger–no crib–for–a bed–
      The li–ttle Lord Je–sus lay down–his sweet–head …

    The GIRLS *continue singing under the following dialogue:*

CONCEPTUA: Delightful, aren't they?

    Beat.

DOLORES: They're not breathing properly.

CONCEPTUA: Mother?

DOLORES: It's the consumption. They weren't tested.

    She whacks a GIRL. *The singing stops.*

You have the consumption, girl?

GIRL: [*under her breath*] I might have *now* …

CONCEPTUA: We're all under strain, Mother.

DOLORES: Hong Kong's burning. They'll surrender.

CONCEPTUA: But it's Christmas!

DOLORES: Oh, Christmas?! The Japs are at mass, of course.

    Planes murmur in the distance. Lights on ROSE *and* LILY *who are spooning a mixture into jam tins.*

CONCEPTUA: Rose is making puddings.

DOLORES: Puddings? What's that recipe, Rose?

ROSE: Half citric acid—from the lemons; half fertiliser—

LILY: From the chickens!

CONCEPTUA: You can't eat *that*?!

ROSE: We don't intend to. It's our latest grenade—I call it the Chin Chicken Chucker, Number 5, Mark 1.

She chucks the grenade to the street. It fizzles disappointingly and gives a sad pop.

Alright—let's work on Mark 2.

CHORUS: [*newsreel-style*] Any man, woman or boy who can throw a brick can hurl a grenade. Get a friend to cycle past towing a pram ... Learn to dig a hole for yourself, lying on your stomach ...

DOLORES: Look! An army of ants—

CONCEPTUA: Scurrying before the storm—

DOLORES: Digging holes—

CONCEPTUA: Looking for shelter—a manger for baby Jesus!

DOLORES: Blowing bon-bons—*bang!*

CONCEPTUA: Wishing on angels—

DOLORES: Kissing beneath the mistletoe as it falls ...

Music: GRACE *plays a melancholy version of 'Away in a Manger'. She wears Ruby's shoes.*

AGNES: [*approaching the doorway*] Good Girl ...

She hovers in the doorway.

What are you doing inside? There's plenty of food.

GRACE *shrugs; keeps playing.*

GRACE: Ruby didn't come.

AGNES: Oh, well. And look how she's missing out!

She enters, with a glass of port and a present.

Did you see your family?

GRACE *shakes her head.*

GRACE: They're long way away. [*Still playing*] They don't know I'm here, I think.

AGNES: Oh. When did you last see them?

GRACE: Four.

AGNES: Four years ago?

GRACE: Four. Where your kids, missus?

Beat.

AGNES: I don't have any.

GRACE: [*nodding*] Might be later, eh?

AGNES *gives a little smile.*

AGNES: Would you like your present?

GRACE: What is it?

AGNES: Close your eyes …

> *She passes the present.* GRACE *opens it—it's a book. She reads the title.*

GRACE: 'Glasses to the Left …'

AGNES: 'Goblets to the Right.' It's the latest handbook from the Savoy!

> *She paws at the book, excited. Finds something …*

[*Reading*] 'A seafood or cocktail fork is always placed to the right of the soup spoon.' [*To* GRACE] Hmm … You learn something new every day. Well, talking of etiquette—I must get back to the guests! *Joyeux Noël,* as they say!

> *She walks away from the unimpressed* GRACE. *As she passes the window, she hesitates.*

There's a light on at Takahashis' …?

GRACE: They're in jail, eh?

AGNES: Internment—they're Japanese. He did a marvellous job on my portrait, though.

> AGNES *leaves.* GRACE *grows curious and goes to the window. She watches the flashing light, a smile growing on her face.*

> *She grabs bits of food and other things while the* CHORUS *chant:*

CHORUS: [*newsreel-style, but gently*] Learn to take advantage of cover. Learn how to stop tanks, and use your weapons. Learn the likely tricks and tactics the enemy will use …

> *The lights flicker and die. In the darkness, we hear* GRACE *whispering loudly:*

GRACE: Ruby?

> *The sound of planes approaching. We hear* AGNES *and* LILY *similarly:*

AGNES: Grace …?

LILY: Rosey?

> *Low light on* DOLORES *and* CONCEPTUA.

DOLORES: Flying ants prefer to die in company.

CONCEPTUA: Mother …?

DOLORES: It's a massacre … all those wings. They're all falling.

CONCEPTUA: Are you not well?

DOLORES: It's Christmas. The girls should sing.

Radio broadcast music.

CHORUS: [*newsreel-style*] The city of Hong Kong has officially fallen.

ROSE *and* LILY *rush in, grenades in hand; they go to the radio.*

After seventeen days of fighting, Allied troops have surrendered.

LILY: *We* won't surrender, hey, Rose?

ROSE: Shhh!

CHORUS: The Japanese commanders paraded their prisoners through the streets. Then they gave the city to their soldiers.

LILY: Dirty Nips!

CHORUS: All Chinese women have been declared prostitutes and free.

The radio static returns.

LILY: We're Australian … hey, Rose?

ROSE *is toying with the grenade.*

ROSE: This won't protect you. [*Breaking*] I promised Mum I'd protect you!

LILY: What about the ARP?!

ROSE: [*shaking her head*] You were right before—I'm not invincible …

She looks around.

We'll have to leave it—all those years of work … Those shelves we made from the gallon drums … Our beautiful silk curtains—I just put them back up! Grandma Tay made those curtains.

LILY: The Yam Yan girls are putting their things on a truck.

ROSE: Where they going?

LILY: Katherine …

Beat.

Rose … imagine if we made a new shop in Katherine—a beautiful one like this! Then, after the war's over, we could easily come back! It would be business as usual—the Katherine branch of the Chin empire!

ROSE *almost smiles.*

ROSE: Look at you, hey. [*Tapping her head*] Got that business head—just like Mum. You got her looks, and her head …

LILY *smiles shyly.*

LILY: What do you think?

Pause.

ROSE: Does anyone sell iced lemon squash in Katherine?

Beat.

LILY: Only *us*! Come on!

She gets up and starts sorting things. ROSE *joins in.*

GIRLS: [*singing/chanting*] The enemy comes to the Territory.
Enemies go with the territory.
Whose is the territory?
And where's the enemy?
We crossed the wire—

A loud plane flies over. The GIRLS *look up, hold their breaths. The plane flies on.*

[*Slowly*] Chop, chop, chop.

Lights crossfade to the post office where a booze-soaked JOAN *sorts the mail.*

JOAN: H.C. White, Mrs Lamb, C. Loydstrommm, Rose Chin … Ooh, that gorgeous J.B. Wills … Mm-mm. Whoops—got a little J.B. Wills in Mrs Lamb. Half her luck. [*Playing with the letters like dolls*] Mrs Lamb, how would you like a little Wills in you? 'Yes, please—I haven't had a scrap of intercourse since The Great War'. There you go … And there *you* go, Rose—pay a visit to Andy Howard—marriageable chap … We should all be friends … Even Takahashi. Someone spent oodles of time writing you a letter—and I'm gonna see that H.C. White fully appreciates it …

BETTY *walks in.*

BETTY: Hong Kong's gone.
JOAN: What?
BETTY: They surrendered.

JOAN: That's terrible …

BETTY: I hope Dad's alright?

JOAN: Dad?

BETTY: In Hong Kong?

JOAN: Oh.

> *Beat.*

Oh, he's probably not there.

> *Pause.*

That letter was ages ago.

> BETTY *sits down.* JOAN *stands.*

I'm going home.

> *Beat.*

BETTY: You're going to the pub.

JOAN: I'm going to the pub … on my way home.

> JOAN *leaves.* BETTY *gazes disinterestedly at the mess of letters. Then an envelope catches her eye. She picks it up, considers.*

CONCEPTUA: Betty … what did we say about reading other people's mail?

BETTY: Mum's drunk.

DOLORES: Her mother's drunk. It's a massacre, all those wings. The secrets are falling …

> BETTY *rips the envelope open.*

BETTY: [*reading*] 'Dear Joan, it's been so long! I miss you so much. Not a day goes by that I don't remember you. Hong Kong's taking a beating. Any day now, we'll go under … Why haven't you written? I'm surrounded by Chinese. Sometimes, it seems I'm the only Englishman around …

> *She falters, then goes to the end.*

'Forever yours, George.' Who the hell's 'George'?

> *She scans the letter.*

'There isn't enough time to record all the stories: dead comrades, wives who abandoned them at home … Joan, we should tell Billy! You could be travelling the world with me! How about London? We'll get you back on the stage ... I want you beside me, dear. I know it's rough on the poor fellow, but Billy's a total loss ...'

BETTY *'s so angry she can't keep reading.*

Thunder claps, wind rips and rain pelts down as the lights flicker and crossfade to CONCEPTUA *and* DOLORES. *The* GIRLS *are jumping up and down at the windows.* DOLORES *is hunched on the floor.* CONCEPTUA *bursts in and shuts the windows.*

GIRLS: We havin' a cyclone, Sister?

CONCEPTUA: Monsoon.

GIRL: Like a baby cyclone?

CONCEPTUA: I suppose.

GIRLS: We're havin' a cyclone!

CONCEPTUA: Shoosh! They're coming to collect us tomorrow, and everybody must help—even you, Alice. Now be a good girl, and start on those dresses.

The GIRLS *starts work to the sound of wind and the rain.*

GIRLS: [*singing/chanting*] Over the garden wall,
    I let the baby fall.
    Then mother came out and gave me a clout,
    And sent me over the wall, the wall, the wall, the wall ...
    [*etc.*]

The GIRLS' *chant continues under the following dialogue:*

DOLORES: We dress for the funeral. We sail the graves.

CONCEPTUA: Lie down, Mother. You're sick.

DOLORES: The horizon isn't constant, you know.

CONCEPTUA: Hush.

DOLORES: Birds aren't nice! They abandon each other! That bird was struggling in the storm. What if she fell?

CONCEPTUA: Birds don't fall, Mother.

DOLORES: She fell! Her wings got caught and she tumbled.

CONCEPTUA: Shoosh.

DOLORES: I abandoned her in a hundred degrees!

CONCEPTUA: [*shaking her head*] It was a seizure!

DOLORES: [*crying*] And she fell ...

The chant dies as DOLORES *wails.*

CONCEPTUA: You weren't to know.

DOLORES: If I was her *real* mother, I would've known! Mothers know these things!

The girls are watching, gobsmacked. CONCEPTUA *takes* DOLORES *in her arms and rocks her.*

CONCEPTUA: Hush now … good girl …

Lights crossfade to Government House where the wind and rain can be heard still squalling.

The dining room is half-packed. GRACE *is wiping a crystal glass.*

AGNES *bowls in, startling* GRACE. *She shuts the door behind her.*

AGNES: Heavens! It's a bad time to move! There's a lake out there.

She takes off her hat and gloves.

Have you finished the crystal?

GRACE *shakes her head and starts wrapping it.* AGNES *walks over, her shoes squelching.*

Singapore's in trouble. Good thing we started early.

GRACE: When we leaving, missus?

AGNES: Monday.

GRACE: What about Ruby?

AGNES: [*shrugging*] She's probably miles away … Have you seen her?

GRACE: I don't think so.

Pause.

AGNES: We can't wait for her … Lord knows we could do with her help, though.

GRACE: You go, missus. I'll wait here.

AGNES: Of course not, girl. The Japs are coming!

GRACE: We can't leave Ruby!

AGNES: She left *us*?!

GRACE: We have to go get her—you have to say 'Sorry'!

AGNES: 'Sorry' for what?!

GRACE: For the dance, missus.

AGNES: That's ridiculous! She knew she wasn't allowed. Everyone was shocked! Now, if she goes off on walkabout, doesn't mean *you* have to lose commonsense. I thought you were a good girl?

GRACE: Well, I'm *not*!

> AGNES *is stunned.*

That's just my stupid name! It's what the nuns called me—'Good Girl'. I had a *proper* name before that—before that day they took me.

> *Beat.*

They were gonna take me to the swings. If I was a good girl ... and let go of my mummy ... they were gonna take me. I never knew they meant forever!

> *Pause.*

My name's Grace ... missus.

RUBY: *Amazing* Grace?

> *A wet and bedraggled* RUBY *walks in.*

GRACE: Ruby?!

> GRACE *leaps up and hugs her.*

RUBY: Gracey Girl.

AGNES: Well, *you've* come home just in time?

> RUBY *stops; gives an icy stare.*

The Japanese ...

> *Silence.*

So, you're coming to Alice?

> AGNES *smiles hopefully.*

RUBY: [*nodding*] With Gracey.

> *Pause.*

AGNES: I'm sorry if there was a ... misunderstanding. We're all clear, now?

RUBY: Yes—clear as that crystal.

> *Beat.*

AGNES: Wonderful! You know, I would've been lost without you.

RUBY: I'm coming for *Grace*.

> *Beat.*

That wasn't clear, madame?

Beat.

AGNES: Perhaps, you don't like me … That's a pity. Perhaps we were … overly familiar. Too long in the tropics—one can go 'native'.

> AGNES *exits, shoes squelching.* RUBY *ruffles* GRACE*'s hair.*
>
> *Lights up on the post office. Air-raid siren.*
>
> BETTY *sits beside a crackly radio, ignoring the air-raid practice.*

CHORUS: [*newsreel-style*] You might be a casualty! During the blackout, someone may tap you on the shoulder and say, 'You're a casualty'. If so, play along with the game, and wait for a stretcher bearer.

> *Crackly music plays.*
>
> JOAN *enters, goes to the light switch.*

JOAN: Air raid, pumpkin …?

> *She turns out the light, plonks down, opens a beer and drinks. A ceiling fan punctuates their silence.*

Are you alright?

> *Beat.*

Hard day at the 'war office'?

> *News broadcast music starts.*

BETTY: Shhh.

CHORUS: [*radio voice*] Prime Minister Curtin has called the surrender of Singapore 'Australia's Dunkirk'. The crushing defeat saw a hundred and thirty thousand captured and nine thousand killed. Meanwhile, Japanese casualties stand at nine thousand killed or wounded …

> BETTY *turns off the radio.*

JOAN: Looks like we're even … nine-all.

> *Pause.*

BETTY: So where's Dad?

JOAN: [*shrugging*] I'm not sure.

> BETTY *waits.*

Alright. They were on their way to Singapore. [*She shrugs.*] That was the last I heard. I don't know. I never hear from him.

Pause.

BETTY: Well ... you're lucky you still get letters, then.

She takes a letter out of her bag and passes it to JOAN.

A nervous musical bass line starts as planes are heard approaching.

Why don't you open it?

Beat.

Go on.

JOAN: I'm not ... sure who it's from.

BETTY: Hong Kong.

JOAN: Hong Kong?

She pulls it out and reads the first line.

'Dear Joan ...'

She unfolds it to find the letter has been hacked. There's nothing left.

Ah.

Beat.

Thanks.

Pause.

The only letter I've had in weeks—

BETTY: How could you *do* that?

She has no answer.

You're married!

Beat.

You're married to my dad!

Pause.

JOAN: I'm sorry, Bett.

Pause.

George cooked for me. That time Billy didn't come back. He cooked ... a beautiful meal ... Billy meant well. He was fun ... but he never thought of things like that. He never took care of me—or you.

BETTY: He was nice!

JOAN: Nice doesn't count! Where was Billy when you were sick or had a busted-up bike? When I went into labour, he wasn't even *here*—he was off at a mate's place, being 'life of the party'.

BETTY: No, Mum. This is all wrong! Were you gonna tell him?

JOAN: Of course.

BETTY: And now we'll never see him again!

> JOAN *swigs at her beer.*

JOAN: Well, you're probably right *there* … He didn't come home for leave, remember? What does *that* tell you, Betty?

BETTY: It tells me he hates you—and I don't blame him!

JOAN: Oh, listen to her, Miss High and Mighty. Spends her days reading other people's mail! People in glass houses …

> BETTY *snatches the beer from her mother, takes a swig. Then she drops it to the floor and stomps outside.* JOAN *calls to her from the doorway.*

Betty—it's dark!

> *Silence.*

Betts …?!

> *She plonks down on the step. The air-raid siren starts.* ROSE, *in ARP gear, bustles in.*

ROSE: [*above the siren*] Excuse me. Are you a casualty?

> JOAN *looks at her.*

> *The siren cuts out. Lights crossfade to* DOLORES *and* CONCEPTUA.

DOLORES: Listen.

> *Silence.*

CONCEPTUA: There's not a sound.

DOLORES: I hear planes.

CONCEPTUA: I hear peace.

DOLORES: The planes are falling!

CONCEPTUA: There *are* no planes. [*Under her breath*] Lord, grant me patience.

DOLORES: Christ have mercy.

Beat.

GIRL: When that boat comin', Sister?

Beat.

They're gonna leave us here, aren't they?

CONCEPTUA: Heavens, no! They're on their way.

DOLORES: The ships burn!

CONCEPTUA: And before you know it, we'll be down south—

DOLORES: The horizon breaks—

CONCEPTUA: Crackling fires, hot cocoa …

DOLORES: —breaks like bones.

CONCEPTUA: Won't that be lovely? Who's all packed, then?

Lights up on ROSE *and* LILY *who are closing the shop.*

DOLORES: Rose and Lily are boarding their windows.

CONCEPTUA: Like a picture theatre!

DOLORES: A tomb. With no ticket out.

Lights up on Government House where a broken AGNES *takes down a picture.*

Mrs Lamb is wrapping her portrait.

CONCEPTUA: Like a gift!

DOLORES: Like a corpse.

GIRL: Her spirit's gone …

CONCEPTUA: Takahashi can't be blamed for that.

GIRLS: It was all his fault!

DOLORES: The light!

CONCEPTUA: The lies!

DOLORES: The crack in the glass—

GIRLS: And no-one could fix it!

DOLORES: Takahashi took a picture—

GIRLS: A dirty picture.

CONCEPTUA: It showed all our weakness—

DOLORES: And Darwin fell like a secret.

DOLORES *wails.*

Lights up on the post office where JOAN *is listlessly sorting mail. It's morning, and a bedraggled* BETTY *walks in.* JOAN *looks up.*

JOAN: He sent you a letter, Bett.

Pause.

Wrong postcode—it's done the rounds.

She hands an envelope to BETTY.

I told you he missed you …

BETTY *looks at the stamp.*

BETTY: Singapore …

She opens the envelope, withdraws the letter; it's pockmarked with holes.

[*Reading*] 'Dear Betty Boop. How's my beautiful princess? We've got to—'

The location has been censored.

Must be Singapore [*Reading on*] '—at last. Bloomin' ship took forever, and I must say, I was crook! It probably doesn't seem like it, but I think about you a lot—wonder how you're getting on, and that. [*She skims a censored line.*] Real sorry I didn't make it there for me leave. I got stuck down the track at a mate's fortieth. I will definitely, *definitely*, see you next time—wild horses and all that. Take care of the old girl for me. I know she's a bit of a handful …'

She searches for more of the letter.

That's it …

JOAN: Fortieth, eh?

BETTY *shakes her head.*

Ah, he probably *tried*. He was always messing up like that.

BETTY *is fighting tears.*

BETTY: That was my last chance to see him!

JOAN: Oh, darlin'—no, no, no. You don't know that! Come 'ere.

She hugs her daughter.

I reckon he'll be alright. Billy, you know—he falls from one disaster to another and, somehow, always makes it through. It's probably that stupid smile, hey—saves his neck.

BETTY *folds the letter, returns it to the envelope.*

You're gonna send a reply, though?

BETTY: What would I say? 'You're a useless git'?!

Pause.

JOAN: Let me think …

She collects paper and pen. Planes murmur gently as they compose.

[*Writing*] Dear Dad … too bad you didn't come home … 'cause you actually missed my wedding! I married a bonza bloke. His name's … Hiroshi Yakomoto.

BETTY: Mum!

JOAN: [*writing*] You don't know him—he's new in town.

BETTY: He flew in one morning and knocked me off my feet.

JOAN: [*writing*] And the rest, they say, is history.

The planes growl louder.

Lights up on DOLORES *and* CONCEPTUA.

DOLORES: Listen—the planes are growling.

CONCEPTUA: It's only an exercise, Mother.

JOAN: [*writing*] He's two foot tall—

BETTY: And two thousand pounds!

JOAN: [*writing*] He didn't walk down the aisle—he *rolled*!

The planes plough onwards. The GIRLS *run inside.*

GIRL: Sister, the tails are red!

GIRLS: The sky is black!

CONCEPTUA: Get under the beds!

JOAN: [*writing*] He's seventy-two.

Beat.

But has great stamina for his age.

BETTY: It's the blood he drinks for breakfast.

JOAN: It's the babies he eats for tea!

DOLORES: Darwin—the sky is breaking! The birds are falling!

GIRLS: The planes are red!

CONCEPTUA: They're not listening to you, Mother. You're the nun who fell off the wall …

GIRLS: [*singing/chanting*] The wall, the wall, the wall.

BETTY: His eyes are black.

JOAN: But his skin's not yellow.

BETTY: Except after drinking.

JOAN: He quaffs champagne with kerosene.

BETTY: I have to mix it for him each night.

JOAN: Or he punishes me with a samurai sword—

> *Beat.*

JOAN/BETTY: And a Betty Bomber!

> *A bomb cracks open the world. The air-raid siren howls. Bombs keep falling.*

CONCEPTUA: Bomb after bomb after bomb!

GIRLS: Blowing churches, pubs, hopes, homes, the picture theatre, the post office.

DOLORES: No-one listened to me. I'm the nun who fell off the wall.

GRACE: The cliffs, sis!

RUBY: The office—it's safer.

GIRLS: [*singing/chanting*] The wall, the wall, the wall …

CONCEPTUA: Hundreds of planes—

DOLORES: From a murderous sun!

GIRLS: [*singing/chanting*] Over the garden wall.

LILY: Let's get in the trench!

ROSE: I have to go help!

LILY: Too late!

GIRLS: [*singing/chanting*] Over the garden wall,
> I let the baby fall …

CONCEPTUA: The might of the Japanese Empire—

DOLORES: Hurled at a tin-shed town.

GIRLS: [*singing/chanting*] Then mother came out,
> And gave me a clout …

> *A bomb whistles.*

DOLORES: It was like cracking an egg with a hammer.

> *A massive bomb explodes. The lights cut out.*

> *Silence.*

In the darkness, a GIRL *starts to sing:*

GIRL: [*singing*] Mother, Mother, I am coming ...

The all-clear siren wails.

GIRLS: [*singing*] Home to Jesus, and to thee,
But my country's hills are distant,
And their lights I cannot see.

Lights find a devastated Government House.

RUBY *struggles out of the rubble.* AGNES *stirs.*

RUBY: Grace ...? All clear!

RUBY *looks around.*

AGNES: Where is she?

RUBY: Grace?

She notices red shoes sticking out of the rubble.

Grace! You right, sis?

She starts to clear the rubble.

We'll get you out. Just tell me—you right?

She tries lifting a beam.

[*To* AGNES] Help!

AGNES: We can't—

RUBY: We have to!

AGNES: Ruby ...

RUBY: Please!

AGNES: [*cracking*] Later! [*Quietly*] We'll get some men and ... we'll bury her later.

RUBY: She's not dead ... she's not dead, you liar! [*Screaming*] Gracey! Grace!

Crying, she collapses beside the shoes.

Lights scan the post office that is now a hole in the ground.

CONCEPTUA: The post office ...? Mother, there's nothing left!

DOLORES: Flying ants prefer to die in company ...

CONCEPTUA: Mother and daughter—both?

DOLORES: They fell.

Pause.

And who will remember their wings?

Pause.

GIRLS: [*quietly*] We will.

> *Lights up on the Chins' where* LILY *is throwing last things into a bag.* ROSE *is lying down.*

CONCEPTUA: The Chins were leaving tomorrow.

DOLORES: A day beyond the horizon.

CONCEPTUA: There's still a chance before the Japs arrive. They're rushing to the train.

DOLORES: Time is cruel. Rose is burnt, and Lily will desert her.

CONCEPTUA: Of course not, Mother! Lily—your sister needs a hospital.

LILY: The hospital's wrecked! Everyone's leaving! [*To* ROSE] Don't worry, Rose. I'll think of something. I'll get a car! Alright? I'm not gonna leave you.

> *Lights crossfade to* CONCEPTUA *and* DOLORES.

CONCEPTUA: Girls, we need to hurry!

DOLORES: We need to hide. I saw two birds abandon a third!

CONCEPTUA: Mother.

GIRL: They goin' without us, Sister?!

DOLORES: Birds aren't nice, you know; they're not nice!

CONCEPTUA: The train is leaving.

GIRLS: They'll leave us behind!

DOLORES: The bomb breaks. The moon bleeds. The cradle—

CONCEPTUA: Mother, would you shut up?! [*Then, with a smile*] Girls …?

> *She ushers the* GIRLS. *A chastised* DOLORES *trails behind.*

> *A train horn toots. A steam engine warms up and departs.*

> *Lights up on the train where the survivors are huddled inside, some asleep.*

That was Katherine … Rose and Lily's new town.

CHORUS: The People's Army …

CONCEPTUA: They'll fight the fight from the riverbank.

DOLORES: Watch for the enemy.

CONCEPTUA: Darwin's a charred memory—
DOLORES: And it's finally safe to bleed.
CHORUS: All of the women are bleeding—
CONCEPTUA: In a simultaneous sigh of relief.
CHORUS: Napkins are delivered.
DOLORES: Mrs Lamb begs like the others—
CONCEPTUA: For a cloth to dam her fears—
DOLORES: While shattered Ruby—
CONCEPTUA: Takes comfort in her loss.
RUBY: It's finally safe to bleed; it's finally safe to breathe. Far from the
    horror of Grace's shoes, it's finally safe to bleed.
CONCEPTUA: The girls' frocks are stained, Mother.
DOLORES: The pain begins …
CONCEPTUA: But fifteen-year-old Maggie Takahashi—
DOLORES: Withers.
CONCEPTUA: She's not bled since she left Darwin.
MAGGIE: How can I trust my blood
    To a bougainvillea friend?
    Sometimes flowering, other times falling.
    Always full of thorns.
CONCEPTUA: Someone has to trust *somewhere* in the world.
DOLORES: How many times should I forgive my enemy?
MAGGIE: Nine thousand times?
CONCEPTUA: Nine thousand times nine thousand. Trust, Maggie.
DOLORES: Bleed.

> *The train is swallowed by the night. The lights fade.*

SCENE TWO

Dry Season, 1946.

Lights build on DOLORES *who's on the convent verandah, investigating
the day.* CONCEPTUA *comes out.*

CONCEPTUA: That's a Dry Season hymn …
DOLORES: Bold as brass, that wind.
CONCEPTUA: We should spend the day outside!
DOLORES: The sun burns.

CONCEPTUA: We'll take an umbrella.

DOLORES: The wind whips it from your grasp. The bough breaks, the cradle rocks—

CONCEPTUA: Rocks.

Beat.

Adelaide was good for you, Mother.

DOLORES: It was the horizon … it never broke.

A skipping rope is turning.

GIRLS: [*chanting*] January, February, March, April …

The skipping rope goes to double time.

CONCEPTUA: Goodness! That must be Maggie Takahashi …

DOLORES: She's eighteen years now …

MAGGIE *sits on her step, fiddling with a tattered camera.* KRISTINA *nervously approaches.*

KRISTINA: Does it work?

MAGGIE: Don't think so.

KRISTINA: Where'd you find it?

MAGGIE: Backyard.

KRISTINA: Are you … by yourself?

MAGGIE: Mum's at the shops. Eddie's in Brisbane.

Beat.

KRISTINA: What about your dad?

MAGGIE: He passed away last year—got sick.

KRISTINA: I'm really sorry, Mags.

MAGGIE *shrugs.*

MAGGIE: He lost his spirit … Must've flown to Japan, eh?

KRISTINA: Mags, I'm sorry. I didn't mean—

MAGGIE: No, you were right—he *was* a spy.

Lights crossfade to the Chins' where ROSE *and* LILY *enter the trashed shop.*

DOLORES: The People's Army are back.

CONCEPTUA: Oh dear. What happened? Were they bombed?

DOLORES *shakes her head.*

DOLORES: The damage was inflicted by our own.

LILY: That makes me wild, Rose—I wouldn't wreck someone else's place!

ROSE: Disgusting …

DOLORES: Well, if their shop was in Chinatown, they'd be looking at a piece of dirt. Razed to the ground.

CONCEPTUA: The enemy?

DOLORES: Enemies come to the Territory. These ones spoke English.

LILY: I suppose *we* were the lucky 'Chinks'.

ROSE: I suppose we were … They smashed our doors and our welcomes—

LILY: Our mirrors and smiles—

ROSE: Our beds, our pillows—

LILY: Our dreams …

> ROSE *notices something strange out the back; she laughs.*

ROSE: But they *left* us something?!

> *Lights crossfade to Government House.*

> RUBY *enters the dining room; notices it's empty.*

RUBY: Her piano!

> AGNES *rushes in, carrying shoes.*

Bloody, stinking mongrels! I'll kill 'em!

AGNES: Oh … oh, how *could* they? She *loved* that piano!

RUBY: There's nothing left now—nothing left of her …

> AGNES *approaches* RUBY; *awkwardly touches her shoulder.*

AGNES: I found these.

> *She holds out Grace's red shoes; brushes the dust clear. She gives them to* RUBY *who presses them to her chest, overcome.*

Dear Grace … I didn't know her like you did, but she was a … she was beautiful.

> *She removes her hat. She coughs and timidly starts to sing:*

> [*Singing*] Amazing Grace …
> How sweet the sound …

> *Lights crossfade to Maggie's.*

MAGGIE: Dad was a spy for the Australian army.

KRISTINA: Oh …

MAGGIE: He cracked codes, translated messages—that sort of thing.

KRISTINA: Why didn't you tell me?

MAGGIE: [*shrugging*] I found out after.

KRISTINA: If I *knew*, I wouldn't have said those things!

MAGGIE: You knew *me*; you knew my *dad*?!

> KRISTINA *lowers her head.*

KRISTINA: Mum said … do youse wanna come for tea?

> MAGGIE *stares at her, then past her.*

MAGGIE: What are the Chins doing?

> *They both stand up.*

KRISTINA: Take a photograph, Maggie!

> *She tries.*

MAGGIE: It doesn't work.

KRISTINA: What if you took that thing off?

> MAGGIE *removes the lens cap and takes a photo as the Chins push a grand piano onto the street.* MAGGIE *and* KRISTINA *run to help. They push it towards Government House where* RUBY *and* AGNES *sing together:*

RUBY/AGNES: [*singing*] I once was lost,
> But now am found,
> Was blind …

ALL: [*singing*] But now … I see.

ROSE: Yoohoo, Mrs Lamb! Don't suppose you lost a piano?!

> *All of the town's women push the piano inside Government House as they sing:*

ALL: [*singing*] 'Twas grace that taught my heart to fear
> And grace my fears relieved;
> How precious did that grace appear,
> The hour I first believed.

> *They gather around the piano.* RUBY *plonks the famous red shoes on its lid.*

CONCEPTUA: Take a photograph, Miss Takahashi.

DOLORES: People will look at this one day. They'll study it with a magni-
fying glass … and they still won't know its secrets.

MAGGIE *takes a photo.*

THE END

Mr Takahashi
and other falling secrets

Sandra Thibodeaux

15–26 February 2017
Brown's Mart Theatre, Darwin

1 March 2017
Godinymayin Yijard Rivers Arts &
Culture Centre, Katherine

30 March–8 April 2017
JUTE Theatre, Cairns

Director
Suellen Maunder

Set and Props Designer
Simone Tesorieri

Costume and Props Designer
Simona Cosentini

Composer
Netanela Mizrahi

Lighting Designer
Rebecca Adams

Production Manager
Angus Robson

Stage Manager
Andi Egan

Performed by **Chenoa Deemal,
Merrilee Mills, Natalie Taylor,
Haylee Wright, Kate Wyvill,
and the ensemble.**

Writer's Note

We think of war as something that happens somewhere else. We see bombing raids on Aleppo and are horrified, although distant. Refugees are people elsewhere, caked in blood and dust, clutching the hands of their children.

While selecting photographs for this publication, I found a number that seemed to belong in the Middle East. But this was us – Darwin people – in 1942, digging our loved ones out from collapsed buildings. It wasn't so long ago. There are people still alive who remember the 19th of February and the long road out of Darwin to somewhere safe.

I started researching and writing this play a few years ago. Some of those who provided assistance were: Garden Point Association & Danila Dilba, Aunty Kathy Mills, NT Library, NT Archives Service, Shellie Morris, Noelle Janaczewska, Peter Matheson, Alex Galeazzi, Gail Evans and various Darwin families whose ancestors' stories inspired some of the play's narrative.

While I uncovered some fascinating facts, the play I wrote is a work of fiction. Historians will detect where I have departed from the official record in search of some deeper truths.

Mr Takahashi turns the lens upon ordinary people caught in the violent storm that was World War II. We are lucky to have escaped from war, while others in the world are still in its grip. I hope that we shall never forget.

Sandra Thibodeaux

Playwright

Like many Australians, I knew the history of World War II but very little about the impact of the war on Australian soil. In Australia, we act as if our country has never been attacked by a force other than the British invasion in the 18th century. I had of course heard about the bombing of Northern Australia, but I had never understood the sheer size of the Japanese force or the impact it had on the civilians who lived through the 64 separate bombing raids that killed over 200 people.

It's not often that stories of war are told solely through the eyes of women. In this beautifully told story, Sandra has woven together the lives of eleven women and a chorus of school children drawn from the cultural melting pot that is Darwin.

The story opens with the daily routines of these women being observed by the nuns of Garden Point. We are introduced to a seemingly harmonious, culturally diverse community but as the threat of war and fear of 'the other' takes over, the racial cracks are exposed.

This is a story of friendship, love, heartbreak, betrayal, regret and fear that reveals a community under pressure. It is a delight for a director.

Suellen Maunder

Director

L: Darwin Post Office. NTAS, C Wilson, NTRS 3335, Item 8.
R: Post Office after the bombing. NTAS, D Clegg, NTRS 234, CP 57/8.

Sandra Thibodeaux
PLAYWRIGHT/COPRODUCER

Sandra is a playwright and poet who has written over a dozen plays that have been produced in Darwin, Indonesia, and elsewhere in Australia. She is currently in pre-production for *The Age of Bones (Jaman Belulang)*. *Mr Takahashi* was shortlisted for the Patrick White Playwrights' Award.

Suellen Maunder
DIRECTOR

Suellen is the Artistic Director and CEO of JUTE Theatre Company and was also one of the founding members of the Company. Suellen is also an actor and director, and has extensive experience in the development and direction of new work. Suellen has directed over 20 new works over the last 25 years.

Mission Church. NTAS, C Wilson, NTRS 3335, Item 213.

Simone Tesorieri
SET & PROPS DESIGNER

Simone is an Italian scenographer born in Bologna. In Australia, Simone has designed for various productions such as *Half & Half*, *Propelled*, *Proper Solid*, *Sentinel Chickens*, *Delirium*, *Stewed*, and *Is my Lipstick on Straight?* Simone is currently working on *My Name is Jimi* and *Here We All are Assembled*.

Simona Cosentini
COSTUME & PROPS DESIGNER

Simona is a Neapolitan scenographer trained in opera, drama and visual arts. She has designed for theatre companies in Queensland and the NT. Recent shows include *Half & Half*, *Propelled*, *Proper Solid*, *Sentinel Chickens*, *Delirium*, *Stewed*, *Is my Lipstick on Straight?* and *Biddigal Dreaming*. Simona is currently working on *My Name is Jimi* and *Here We All are Assembled*.

Netanela Mizrahi
COMPOSER

Netanela is a multi-instrumentalist, composer and music educator. She is the principal violist of the Darwin Symphony Orchestra and co-founder of chamber group the Ad Hoc Ensemble. In 2017 Netanela is creating new works for sitar, voice and chamber ensemble to be performed in Darwin's WWII Oil Storage Tunnels.

Rebecca Adams
LIGHTING DESIGNER

Rebecca is an architect and theatre designer. She doesn't remember the bombing of Darwin but she once met someone who did. Rebecca has worked in theatre lighting in Melbourne for 15 years. Recent productions include *Jehovah's One Table Restaurant*, *When The Rain Stops Falling*, *The Glass Menagerie*, *And I'm The Queen Of Sheba*, *Contagion's Kiss* and *God of Carnage*.

Angus Robson
PRODUCTION MANAGER

Angus is a Darwin-born production manager who has spent the last five years toiling away in the darker corners of various theatres and has loved every minute of it. He has worked with Tracks Dance, Brown's Mart Theatre and Corrugated Iron Youth Arts, amongst others. Angus loves working with other people's art and taking ideas from sketches to stage.

Chenoa Deemal
RUBY

Chenoa holds a Bachelor of Fine Arts (Acting). She has been working professionally as an actor since 2009, with shows including *Rainbow's End, Mother Courage and Her Children, The 7 Stages of Grieving* and *A Man with Five Children*. She will perform *The 7 Stages of Grieving* in London later this year at Origins: Festival of First Nations.

Andi Egan
STAGE MANAGER

This will be Andi Egan's 31st stage management role across Australia and the US. In 2016 she stage managed *Broken, When the Rain Stops Falling* & *And I'm the Queen of Sheba*. She studied Applied Theatre at Griffith University.

Merrilee Mills
MRS AGNES LAMB / JOAN

Merrilee is a theatremaker, musician, composer and arts educator. She holds degrees in music, education and performance, and is currently undertaking her Masters in Applied Theatre. Her recent work includes direction of Andrew Bovell's *When the Rain Stops Falling*, and the multi-artform collaboration 'MOVED' for Darwin Festival.

Natalie Taylor
SISTER CONCEPTUA

Natalie has worked in Australia, New Zealand and the UK. Career highlights include *At Sea Staring Up, Junk Rooms, Fools Gold, Property Search TV, Hate Ate It, Underbelly* and much more. Natalie has been a part of the JUTE family for many years.

Haylee Wright
GRACE

Haylee graduated from high school in 2016, and this is her first professional performance. Previously she has performed in *The Violent Outburst That Drew Me to You* by Finegan Kruckemeyer and *Once Upon A Mad House*.

Kate Wyvill
MOTHER DOLORES

Kate is a playwright, actor, director and producer. She trained as an actor at the Q Theatre, Penrith, and has performed in the UK and Australia. Recent theatre credits in Darwin include Annette, *God of Carnage* (2013) and Amanda, *Glass Menagerie* (2015).

PRODUCTION NOTE:

Mr Takahashi *featured professional and non-professional cast members. Darwin and Cairns productions engaged different non-professional actors, some of whom were not confirmed before this publication went to print. Due to this, the professional actors only are listed.*

Corrugated Iron Youth Arts

Corrugated Iron Youth Arts delivers artistic programs that inspire young people and unleash creative young minds. Corrugated Iron's broad program includes professional productions, community engagement, performances, training and mentoring. Corrugated Iron works across the Top End of the Northern Territory, and projects take the company further afield – intrastate, interstate and internationally.

Mr Takahashi is a wonderful project for Corrugated Iron as it provides an opportunity for early career artists and young creatives to work alongside creative professionals in a production that tells an important story of Northern Australia.

CORRUGATED IRON YOUTH ARTS STAFF

Jane Tonkin, Fiona Carter, Samara Erlandson, Nikki Jeffries, Tierney White, Jody Reichstein, Hemlock Mejarne

JUTE Theatre Company

Established in Cairns in 1992, JUTE Theatre Company is a major regional theatre company driving the development, co-production and national touring of contemporary Australian plays from the regions. JUTE is a house of ideas and action that exists to fan the fire in the bellies of regional theatre artists.

JUTE THEATRE COMPANY STAFF

Suellen Maunder, Karen Engel, Amanda Bellanger, Peta Cooke.
Graphic Designer: Tim Cooke – Design Disrupt

Special Thanks

To all of our families and friends.

Brown's Mart, Sean Pardy, Kelly Blumberg, Kerrin Schallmainer, and Jessie Davis.

Lord Mayor Katrina Fong Lim, City of Darwin, Anna Malgorzewicz, and Kylie Salisbury.

Cairns City Council.

Territory Remembers, Jenny Deveraux.

Gail Evans, Knock-em-Down Theatre.

The volunteer cast members, their families and schools/workplaces.

Rebecca Harris and the actors who performed in the 2012 reading.

Franck Gohier, Jett Street, Will Roberts, Tim Cooke and Will Tinapple.

Cavenagh Theatre Trust, Peg Gellert.

Rachel Tumminello.

Theatre Kimberley.

Gwen Knox.

Australian Government
Catalyst—Australian Arts and Culture Fund

Australia Council for the Arts

Australian Government
Festivals Australia

Australian Government
Department of Communications and the Arts

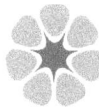

ANZAC Centenary QUEENSLAND

Queensland Government

Proudly sponsored by
NORTHERN TERRITORY GOVERNMENT

BROWNS MART THEATRE

TERRITORY REMEMBERS 75 YEARS
Commemorating the Bombing of Darwin and defence of Northern Australia

75TH ANNIVERSARY

CITY OF DARWIN

Southern Cross TELEVISION

COMMUNITY BENEFIT FUND
Helping Build Better Communities

THE TERRITORY REMEMBERS
75 YEARS

Commemorating the Bombing of Darwin
and defence of Northern Australia

Honouring our wartime history

HELL-F
CORN

www.territoryremembers.nt.gov.au

NORTHERN
TERRITORY
GOVERNMENT

www.ingramcontent.com/pod-product-compliance
Lightning Source LLC
Chambersburg PA
CBHW050022090426
42734CB00021B/3382